BUS

This Book Is Presented To

_____

By

_____

_____

_____

_____

Acknowledgments

In my deepest, most personal way, I want to thank my God and Lord, Jesus Christ. Without Him, nothing in my life would have been possible. Even if it was, it would not have amounted to anything lasting. To Him go all of the honor, glory and credit. Go God!

The following people have made a great impact on this book and my life – I thank them very much: My lovely wife, Kim, and both of our wonderful kids, Jack and Matthew, my brother, Lawrence, my parents, Ward, David, Sandy, Jean, Mark Abernathy from Capstar Lending, Jim, Millie, Emily, Ken White, Jay Robinson, Gordy Cross, and all of the people with which I have shared time, thoughts, events and love. To all of them, I say thank you and may God bless you more than you can imagine, expect or pray for.

The Ultimate Home Buyer's Book

The World's Best Book For Buying Homes & Shopping Loans

Wade Grassedonio

Bigger Picture Publishing

Bigger
Picture
Publishing

Bigger Picture Publishing
PMB 394
14493 SPID
Corpus Christi, TX 78418

ISBN 0-9776310-0-1

DISCLAIMERS

The practice of real estate and its laws vary from state to state and area to area. The information contained in this book may not be representative of all laws, ordinances, customs, practices and the like. Rely upon your real estate professional, loan officer, attorney etc...for advice concerning your area and purchase.

This book is a general guide and may not be accurate for specific situations. There may be mistakes in content, spelling, wording or otherwise. Do not use this book as a replacement for an attorney, real estate professional, or profession loan officer/mortgage broker. Do not use this book as your sole source of information when purchasing a home. Seek the advice of professionals whenever possible.

This book is intended to help the average person educate themselves as to the basics of the home buying process. It is not intended to be used as a legal guide in any way, shape or form.

Do not rely on the information contained in this book to execute your home purchase. Use it as a reference guide for basic knowledge. Your loan officer, attorney and agent will help you with details.

If you do not wish to be bound by the above, you may return this book to the publisher for a full refund.

GUARANTEE

Bigger Picture Publishing offers an unconditional money back guarantee. At any time, if you do not think this book was of any benefit to you, please return it to the author for a full refund. There is no time limit on this offer.

2 Books In One

1. Quick Reference Guide
Carry it with you throughout the home buying process.

2. A Regular Book
Read it in its entirety before you shop for a home. It will give you a great base of knowledge from which to draw. If you have any questions or comments, please feel free to email me - ultimatehomebuyersbook@yahoo.com

Special Bonus Chapter

CHAPTER 2
Developing A Vision For What You Need

To find your ideal home and loan, work through Chapter 2. By answering all of the questions as honestly as possible, in writing, you will sift your way through the confusion and arrive at a clear cut picture for where you are, where you want to be and how to go about reaching your objectives.

Index

Read chapters 2 and 21...even if you don't read anything else!

1

8 Steps Of The Home Buying Process

Average time frame: 30 days

1. Get Pre-Approved – Have a loan officer analyze your income, debts and assets to determine the price range and monthly payments you can afford. This will help you avoid the agony of falling in love with a home for which you cannot qualify.

2. Find a real estate agent – It is important to find a real estate agent that is willing to work hard, listens well, answers questions without making you feel funny and is knowledgeable about the area in which you are looking. You must be able to trust your agent absolutely and get along with them easily. Your friends and your loan officer are great sources for names of good real estate agents.

3. Find a Home – This is the fun part. Enjoy your time with your real estate agent.

4. Get a Home Under Contract – When you find a home you love, get it under contract. The phrase "under contract" means to make an offer and have it accepted by both the buyers and sellers. Make sure you get an option period of at least seven to ten days, if possible. An option period, also called a feasibility period, allows the buyers to inspect the home, their financing etc…and make sure they still want to fulfill the transaction.

5. Lock the Rate – Once the home is under contract, call your loan officer and make him aware of the situation. If market conditions indicate, your loan officer may suggest that you lock your interest rate. "Locking the interest rate" means that your interest rate will be set for a given period of time. This is advantageous in a rising interest rate environment.

6. Give Information to the Lender – Your lender will need specific information from you (See Ch. 6). If you work well with your lender, life will be easy. If you don't, life will…(well, we won't even talk about that). What does it mean to 'work well' with your lender? Tell your lender everything they need to know, as honestly as possible AND provide the information they request QUICKLY!

7. Do the GRUNT Work – Don't worry! Your real estate agent and loan officer will guide you through this. This part of the process will include a survey, appraisal and inspections, repairs etc.

8. Go to Closing – Once all of the above is done and everyone is happy, you go to the title company, attorney or escrow officer for closing. Once there, you will sign a huge stack of papers, deliver a check and own your new home. Three important things about closing are; the check must be a cashier's check made out to the correct party, you must bring a picture ID and you may not get the keys to your new home until the loan funds (the money actually passes from the lender to the title company). Funding may be immediate, take a few hours, or sometimes, a few days. Ask your agent and loan officer for projections as to your situation.

CONGRATULATIONS!!!

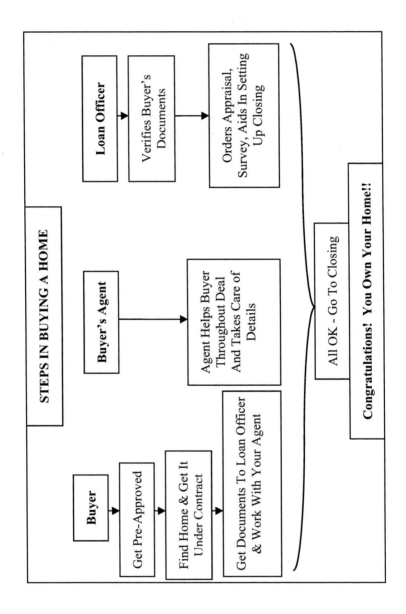

STEPS IN BUYING A HOME

Buyer
- Get Pre-Approved
- Find Home & Get It Under Contract
- Get Documents To Loan Officer & Work With Your Agent

Buyer's Agent
- Agent Helps Buyer Throughout Deal And Takes Care of Details

Loan Officer
- Verifies Buyer's Documents
- Orders Appraisal, Survey, Aids In Setting Up Closing

All OK - Go To Closing

Congratulations! You Own Your Home!!

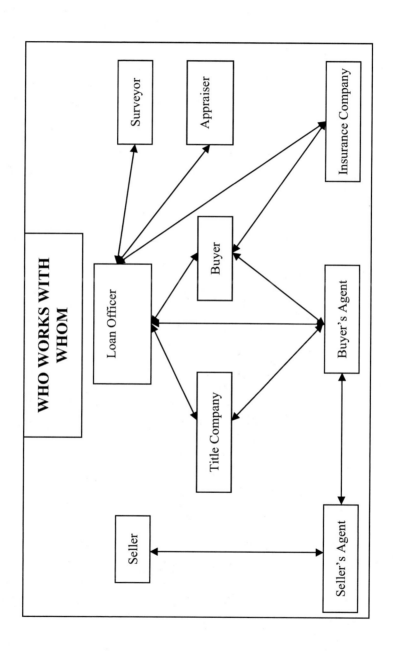

2

Developing A Vision For What You Need!

Buying a home is the biggest investment most people make in their lives. The decisions they make during the process affect them for many years. How do most people make these important decisions? With respect to the home, they usually ponder and scrutinize carefully. With respect to the loan, they frequently jump into the first home loan that comes along, usually the 30 year fixed rate. Why? Because it is the only loan of which they have heard and probably the one their friends or family members suggested.

Friends and family are great, but since this may be the biggest investment of your entire life, it is worth a little bit of your time to consult a professional when it comes to a home loan.

Come up with clear financial goals and investigate the loan programs that are available to help you achieve them. There are many that you may not have heard about. A loan is a tool that, if used wisely, can help you reach your financial goals. It is not just something you pay each month.

Work through the following questions and, when finished, you should have a clear picture for the home and loan that will best suit your needs. Write the answers on a separate piece of paper. You will need them at the middle and end of this process. Share the final information with your loan officer and real estate agent and they will do their best to make it a reality.

Mortgage

How quickly do you want to move into your new home?

Less than 30 days:	Be prepared to work quickly.
30 - 45 days:	Normal
60 – 75 days:	Interest rate may be slightly higher
than	the 45 day move-in.
Over – 75 days:	Costs may be incurred to lock the interest rate and the interest rate may be slightly higher than the 45 day move-in.

What is the most important thing to you with respect to a home loan?

(See below for sample answers)

This question usually leaves everyone blank because they never think about it. *It is, however, the most important question* you can ask yourself. Answer this question in any manner that applies to you. You do not have to use one of

the sample answers below. Consider the answer well
before writing it down.

Sample Answers

Lowest monthly payment possible, lowest interest rate
possible, tax advantages, the length of time you will live in
the home (3 – 5 years), need help building retirement, you
want to pay it off as fast as possible, you will be making
large payments to principal, etc….

**How much money do you have available for a down
payment, closing costs and pre-paid expenses?**

**What is the maximum monthly payment with which
you will be comfortable?**

How long do you plan to live in the home?

What is your credit score?

> The type of loan and interest rate can be affected by
> your credit score. Following is a rough credit score
> guideline:
>
> 720 or above: Excellent ++
> 700 – 719:   Excellent
> 680 – 699:   Good to Very Good
> 660 – 679   Average – Good
> 620 – 659   Shaky - Average
> 600 – 619   Might have some problems
> 599 – or below   There will be problems, but
>   they may be able to be
>   overcome.
>
> (See Chapter 12 for information on how to get free
> copies of your credit report) If you do not know
> your credit score, your loan officer can tell you after
> your credit is checked.

What are your retirement goals versus your present situation?

Ready to retire
Almost ready to retire
I have a little saved up
I need drastic help
Don't know (talk to a financial advisor soon or you'll be kicking yourself sooner than you think.)

QUICK QUALIFICATION

How much do I qualify for?

(Incorrect English, I know, but this is the way everyone says it in real life.) Here is a quick calculation that will give you a 'ballpark' figure for the amount for which you qualify. This depends on credit, loan programs, loan amounts, etc... A pre-qualification is not the same as a pre-approval. Please see Chapter 11 for definitions and differences.

✓ Gross monthly income (before taxes)
(all borrowers combined): _____

✓ Multiply it by 49%   X   .49

✓ Write the answer on this line   _____
✓ Subtract the monthly payments
listed on your credit report   -_____

✓ **This number is the maximum**_____
monthly payment you will be able to handle by standard means of pre-qualification. This number *includes principal, interest, monthly taxes, monthly insurance and mortgage insurance, if applicable.* Ask the real estate

agent or loan officer to translate this into a home price for the area in which you want to buy.

Now that you have worked through this, put your answers together. Here is one possible example: I want to move into my new home in 30 days. The most important thing to me with respect to a home loan is, the fact that I will only live in the house for 3 years. I have $10,000 for a down payment, closing costs, and pre-paid expenses. The maximum monthly payment I will be comfortable with is $1,500 and I am 'quick qualified' for a payment of $1,700. My credit score is a 700 and I am about half way to where I want to be financially when I retire.

Write your scenario out in paragraph form and share it with your loan officer. He'll love you for it, I promise.

Home
(Write out the answers just as you did above)

In what type of neighborhood do you want to live?

Do you want to be close to schools, shopping, medical facilities etc.?

How many square feet do you want in your new home?

Would your ideal home be one, two or three stories?

How many bedrooms?

How many bathrooms and half baths?

How many cars will you put in the garage?

Do you want a pool?

What size yard do you want?

Do you want brick, wood, stucco, other?

What is the most important thing to you when it comes to your new home?

Do you want a condominium, town-home or single family residence?

Do you care if the garage is in front or back?

Do you want certain rooms to be large?

Now, summarize the Home section in much the same way as you did the Mortgage section – including the amount for which you qualify. Tell it to your real estate agent, and after you pick them up off of the floor, they will wipe away tears of joy, thank you for being able to relay the information so clearly and then get to work for you.

3

Should I Rent Or Should I Own?

If you are currently renting and wondering if you can afford a home, chances are…You Can!! And, you can probably own a larger home than you think.

The major factor that affects the price of the home you can afford is the income tax deduction you will get for the interest you pay on your mortgage. Your monthly payment may be higher than it is now, but the money you save on taxes will make up for it at the end of the year. Look at the example below and I think you will be amazed at how much better off you will be owning a home rather than renting a home.

Example

Assumptions:

Yearly Property Tax Rate	2 %
Yearly Insurance Rate	.5%
Income Tax Bracket	28%
Current Rent Payment	$1,250

Home That Can Be Purchased For The Associated Rent

Price	$210,000
Loan Amount	$189,000
Down Payment	$21,000
Monthly Payment	$1,634
Yearly Tax Savings	$4,602
Monthly Tax Savings	$384

Scenarios Compared

Current Rent:	$1250	Home Payment	$1634
Tax Savings	$0	Tax Savings	$ 384
Net Payment	$1250	Net Payment	$1250

In this example, you can see that paying $1,634 per month for a house payment is equivalent to paying $1,250 per month in rent once you take into account the yearly savings on your income taxes. This means if you own the home described above, you will be able to pay $4,602 LESS per year in taxes. This savings makes up for the increased monthly payment. (As usual, consult an accountant for details)

In addition to this, by owning a home, you will build equity over time. The home in the example above would be worth far more in 30 years assuming that it appreciates over time like most homes do. If this home appreciates at just 2% per year, in 30 years it will be worth $380,385. Let's do some more math. The following example is a look at a likely financial situation at the end of thirty years.

	Renting	**Owning**
Equity	$0	$380,385
Tax Savings	$0	$138,000
Financial Advantage	**$0**	**$518,385**

So...you tell me....is it better to buy or rent?!

4

Avoiding The Most Common Mistakes

This is probably the biggest investment of your life. Do it as wisely as possible. Below are eleven things that will help keep you on track. This, however, is not everything.

1. Make Sure Everything Is In Writing – In a nutshell, if it is not written down, it is not real and cannot be relied upon or enforced. That is why we have contracts.

2. Inspect The Home – Have a home inspection done and, if necessary, have a termite inspection too. Go over the reports in detail. If it is a condominium or townhouse, look at the homeowner's association rules and regulations. Ask your real estate agent to look over the information and let you know if they see anything of concern.

3. See It For What It Is – Don't be impressed by nice furniture. Unless you are buying the furniture too, it will be gone.

4. View Several Homes - See at least 4 properties. Don't jump into the first property you see (unless you know it is *perfect*). Your real estate agent will show you enough properties to give you a good overall feel for the market.

5. Let The Professionals Help – You have a team of people working for and with you. These include your loan officer, real estate agent, title insurance agent, insurance agent and so forth. Ask them for guidance. Ask questions whenever they come up, but give them room to work too. They know their job and will be of great value to you.

6. Make Use Of The "Final" – The final walk through, which is done just before closing, is to make sure the property is vacant, clean and any agreed upon repairs have been made. Look at everything and make sure it conforms to the details of the contract.

7. Investigate Costs – Look at all costs before you sign. These things include but are not limited to; closing costs, taxes, insurance, repairs, maintenance projections, homeowner's dues, utility bills, etc.

8. Mortgage Payment – When considering your mortgage payment, take into account living expenses, income level and future expenses like children, furniture, repairs etc…

9. Plan - Closing dates sometimes change – even though every effort is made to stay on schedule. Make sure that you have a place to stay while the transaction winds up. A late closing can be irritating and inconvenient, but if everyone does their job and keeps their cool, chances are everything will work out just fine.

10. **Be Loyal** – Take the time to find the right real estate agent and loan officer with which to work. Once you have chosen them, be loyal. If you are, they will work very hard for you. If you are not loyal, they will lose their incentive and your home-buying experience may become a nightmare.

11. **Get Pre-Approved** – Many home sellers will not enter into a contract until they have a letter from a lender stating that you have been pre-approved for a loan. A pre-approval will also help you know a realistic price range and make your home shopping a much more pleasurable experience.

5

What To Look For In An Agent, Loan Officer And...You!

LOAN OFFICER

1. HONESTY – If I need to explain this one, we have problems.

2. SERVICE - "What Does *Service* Mean When It Comes To A Mortgage?" **This is an actual question asked by a real customer.**

People think mortgages are all the same and all that matters is a great rate. Unfortunately, **that is *far* from the truth.**

When it comes to a mortgage, service counts for a lot. Service means; competitive rates, on-time closings, the ability to contact your loan officer at any time, loan products and advice that help you reach your financial goals, education concerning the loan process, and much more.

Think of it this way. Would you go to a restaurant if you knew that you would end up waiting forever to get your food, your drinks would run dry, the food would be cold and the waiter would be rude.....just because it was cheap! No, of course you wouldn't. Service Counts!

Mortgage Nightmare

Company A promises unbelievably low rates, fees etc... During the process, the borrower (you) cannot reach your loan officer and everything falls through the cracks. Closing is delayed - the seller, agents and borrower (you) get mad and the people buying your house threaten to back out of the deal. When closing finally does come, the fees and/or rate are much higher than expected. After the transaction the borrower (you) are upset, unsatisfied and have much less money in the bank. Later, the borrower (you) have some questions or problems but the loan officer can't be reached to solve them - the problem continues...DON'T LET THIS HAPPEN TO YOU!

3. **COMPETITIVE RATES** – Shop around and see what kind of deals you can find. Many times it is better to go with the competitive rate rather than the absolute cheapest. Remember, there are lots of companies and people that are trying to sucker you into a deal. Everything they told you will change at the last minute and they are hoping that you will be too weary to drop them and start over with someone else. Check references too.

4. **REASONABLE CLOSING COSTS** – Cheapest is not always best. You usually get what you pay for. Refer to the 'mortgage nightmare' described above. Shop around and see what you can find. Remember, if you cut out all of

the costs, you cut out the loan officer's incentive to do the best job possible for you. The difference in service will probably not be intentional, but it may be there. Think of it in terms of yourself. What kind of incentive would you have if you had to work for free? Treat others like you want to be treated.

5. THE ABILITY TO EDUCATE WITHOUT MAKING YOU FEEL UNCOMFORTABLE – The loan officer should be able to explain everything in a way so as to educate you and make you feel comfortable. If they are a 'fast talker' or talk down to you, leave them.

6. DESIRE TO WORK FOR YOU – Look for someone that is driven to do the best job possible.

7. MARKET KNOWLEDGE – A good loan officer should have access to real-time market data, be up to date on the news, know when the next economic reports are due and have access to many loan programs.

REAL ESTATE AGENT

1. HONESTY – This is by far the most important factor. Everything else hinges on it.

2. DESIRE TO WORK FOR YOU – Look for an agent that is really interested in working for you. If you are "just another deal", move on to someone else.

3. MARKET KNOWLEDGE – A good real estate agent will know the area and the homes that are located within that area. They will also know market trends and educate you as to what you need to know and what to avoid.

4. EXPERIENCE – Well seasoned brokers and agents are always an excellent resource because of the vast amounts of schooling and experience they possess. If, however, you find a "new" real estate agent that has the first three items in this list and the STRONG backing of their manager and co-agents, it may be wise to use them. Many times they do an excellent job.

5. TENACITY – You want someone who will stick to it until the bitter end. Sometimes real estate transactions get very difficult and you need an agent who will hang in there and fight for what is right. You will love the results.

6. AVAILABILITY – You need an agent that will meet with you when you are available. This is very important. You must also be able to reach them whenever you call.

YOUR RESPONSIBILITIES!!!

YES YOU READ IT RIGHT. *YOU* HAVE RESPONSIBILITIES TO YOUR LOAN OFFICER AND REAL ESTATE AGENT TOO!!

1. BE HONEST – If you are not honest you might as well get a tub full of misery and start wallowing in it. Even if you are a "little fuzzy" on the facts, you are asking for trouble. Be honest and up front with everyone and everything. The truth WILL come out, period.

2. BE RESPECTFUL – Respect the real estate agent's and loan officer's time, work load and stress factor. Believe it or not, they are doing the best job possible and *they do not get paid until the transaction closes and funds.* The old rule of thumb applies; treat others how you want them to treat you.

3. BE PROMPT – Be prompt with respect to delivering information and arriving at meetings. The more you do this, the better your life will be.

4. MOTIVATE – Yes, you can motivate real estate agents and loan officers. The best ways to motivate them are; do what you say when you say you will do it, be honest and respectful and deliver the information that is requested as soon as possible. When you do these things, you come across as a professional and everyone likes to work with a professional.

5. LOYALTY – Be loyal to your real estate agent and it will come back to "bless" you. Remember the golden rule, "treat others like you want to be treated."

6

Information Your Loan Officer Will Need

Following is the basic information your loan officer will need for a standard "full documentation" loan. This is a 'worst case scenario'. There is a good chance you will not have to provide this much information. **The items in bold, however, are needed with almost every application.**

A copy of your driver's license

Name and phone number of the insurance agent you will use for this purchase

Social security number

Address history for two years

Employment history for two years with addresses and phone numbers

Up to two years W-2's

Up to two years 1099's

Up to two years SIGNED income tax returns

Up to two months bank statements – all pages required, even blank pages

Most recent statement from investment accounts such as mutual funds, IRA's, etc…all pages required, even blank pages

Listing of all real estate owned. For each property provide address, type of property (single family residence, duplex, condominium, townhouse, etc.), current value, current loan balance, current payment with taxes and insurance included and monthly income received.

Copy of divorce decree, if applicable

Copy of Social Security Award letter, if applicable

Copy of bankruptcy discharge, if applicable

If you are doing a VA loan you will need discharge papers and your DD-214

You may need to pay for the appraisal, application fee, and other items at application

7

Real Estate Agents: Their Job, Their Pay, and Who They Represent

One of the first things you should ask your agent is who they represent. It can be a very confusing issue. They can either represent the buyer, the seller or both. Sometimes, they may not have a choice depending on which company has rights to a particular listing. Their representation may have to change during the process too, depending on which house you select and who has the listing. Your agent should be open and up front with this information.

Ideally, you want a real estate agent to represent you and your interests. If something does change during the process and they can no longer represent you, it is still possible to finish the deal and be in great shape. Just ask questions as they arise. Remember, be honest and loyal and they should do the same.

Real estate agents do not get paid until the deal closes. They do so much more work than you think, it is amazing. They put up with huge amounts of stress. DO NOT 'use' them, make them do a lot of work and then go with another agent. That is a slap in the face. You would not want it done to you, so do not do it to them. They earn their money! If, however, the agent is not doing their job or is doing a very poor job, change immediately.

Most people who are not real estate agents think that it is an easy job. They think you just show a few houses, sign a few papers and collect a fat check. That couldn't be further from the truth. I have seen many people become agents because they think it will be an easy way to make a living. All of them get the shock of their lives when the demands and stress of the job become real. At that point they either become dedicated, hard working professionals or quit. Most of them quit.

So, chances are you are working with a dedicated professional who is trying their best to make the process easy for you by taking the "hits" themselves. Work with them, not against them.

Do not cut an agent's commission to get a "good deal." It crushes their loyalty and motivation. Think about it in terms of yourself. Would you take a pay cut to give someone else a "good deal?" And if you would - be honest - you would be resentful. They are human too. Let them make a living. They earn it!

As far as the 'fat check' goes, only in rare cases do they get to keep the entire commission. Usually it is split between two companies and then further split between the company and the individual agent with whom you work. They don't get as much as you think.

If you don't believe me...become a real estate agent. You'll agree with me sooner than you think.

8

Internet, Television and Radio Mortgage Companies

WARNING!!! **These guys can be the definition of** *scam artists.* **In my career I have bailed out more borrowers from these kinds of mortgage companies than I care to count.**

Many times their very business model is set up to account for a huge number of people rejecting them after they find out the true costs and hardships of working with them. How do they do this...by making enough money off of the people who actually complete the loan process to pay for the ones that reject them. What does this mean to you? It means an expensive, difficult loan. After all, the people who use them pay enough to make up for all of the people who back and still give the company a hefty profit.

The normal complaints are:

They don't close on time!

They don't close at all!

They take forever!

They make up for the low rates by charging huge fees!

They don't show you those huge fees until just before closing!

You are a just a number and they don't care about you!

They sucker you in with unbelievable rates, terms and/or closing costs and then either change everything at the last minute or charge huge fees!

The typical scenario:

The borrower shops around like he is supposed too, and gets suckered into the unbelievable rates and low fees of the internet, radio and TV companies. He goes through the process only to have it turn into a nightmare and take a really, really long time and huge amount of work. The borrower must then decide to either finish it with that company and take the financial and emotional hits, or find any loan officer who can help quickly. In either scenario he will have to settle for a deal that is not as good as what he was quoted before he started the process.

Forego the misery. Get a good faith estimate that is a worst case scenario and a loan officer that is honest and up front about everything.

9

Good Faith Estimates

A good faith estimate, or GFE, is an estimate of all costs and the projected monthly payment associated with the loan. Get a GFE, in writing, from any lender you are interested in using.

ITEMS AND COSTS WILL VARY FROM REGION TO REGION!

What To Look For – Look for detailed information that spells out the monthly payment and all costs clearly. It should designate closing costs, pre-paid expenses, loan-to-value, loan type, cash from/to borrower etc...

WARNING!!!
Since this is only an "estimate" many lenders, especially the ones that offer ridiculously low rates and closing costs, will change the figures (always upward) just before closing. The thinking is that once you finally get to closing, you will

go on and pay the extra money and close the deal rather than start all over again with another lender.

What you want is a GFE that is a 'worst case scenario' so, if it does change, it will reduce your costs.

Compare GFE's from different lenders. See if you can find any items that are on one and not the other. Then, if you do, ask each loan officer why it is that way. The thing that makes them hard to compare is that one fee can go by many different names. Do your best, it could save you lots of money.

Do not go with the lowest GFE simply because it looks like it is the least expensive. Make sure it is complete and, hopefully, a worst case scenario. If you don't, plan on *big, unpleasant* surprises at the end.

Typical Items Included In A Good Faith Estimate

CLOSING COSTS

Bank Fees: Origination fee, Discount point, Credit report fee, Underwriting fee, Lender closing fee, Processing fee, Settlement fee, etc…

Title Company Fees: Flood certificate, Document preparation, Attorney's fees, Title insurance, Recording fee, City/County Taxes/Stamps, State Taxes/Stamps, Endorsements, Courier fees, etc…

Miscellaneous Fees: Appraisal, Survey, Pest Inspections, Home Warranty, etc…

PRE-PAID EXPENSES

These fees include; pre-paid Interest, first year insurance premium, several months of escrows for insurance, several months of escrows for taxes, escrows for Home Owners Association Dues, etc... (Escrows are also known as impounds)

DOWN PAYMENT

MONTHLY PAYEMNT

First mortgage, Second mortgage (if any), Insurance, Taxes, Mortgage Insurance, Home Owners Association Dues, etc...

CASH TO/FROM BORROWER

MISCELLANEOUS CHARGES OR FEES

10

All About Monthly Payments

Your monthly mortgage payment is made up of the following items: principal, interest, taxes, insurance and mortgage insurance. Depending on the loan program and down payment, some of those items may not be included. Note, however, that even if you do not have to pay taxes and insurance as part of your monthly payment, you will have to pay them in full when they are due. So….save for it!

Following is an example of a mortgage payment with all the bells and whistles.

Home Value	$130,000
Loan Amount	$123,500
Interest Rate	6%
Term	30 years

Payment Information

Principal and Interest	$ 740.44
Taxes	$ 180.00
Insurance	$ 90.00

| Mortgage Insurance | $ 80.28 |
| Total | $1,090.72 |

Taxes and insurance will vary widely from one state or area to another. Check with your real estate agent for local tax and insurance rates.

The Significance of 20% Down

If your down payment is 20% or more of the purchase price, you do not have to pay mortgage insurance or include taxes and insurance in your monthly payment.

If your down payment is less than 20% of the purchase price, you *must* pay mortgage insurance *and* include taxes and insurance in your monthly payment.

There are, however, two ways around this predicament. The first is to go with a "first and second" loan scenario and the second is to go with a sub-prime loan. Both of these programs are discussed in detail in Ch. 14, Types Of Loans And Their Uses.

11

Pre-Qualified Vs. Pre-Approved

Rule #1: Always get pre-approved *before* you go look for a house. It is not only fair to you and your real estate agent, but will save you huge amounts of emotional pain.

Sellers, many times, will not accept an offer unless the buyer has already been pre-approved by a lender.

Things to Understand

Both pre-qualifications and pre-approvals are heavily based on ratios. The ratios that are taken into consideration are the front or first ratio and the back or second ratio. The first ratio is the percentage of your income that is used up by your projected house payment. The second ratio, which is the most important, is the percentage of income that is used up by the projected house payment plus all of the monthly debts listed on the credit report. Lenders and laws put limits and restrictions on how high those ratios are allowed to go.

Pre-Qualification – A pre-qualification, as shown below, is nothing more than a mathematical computation that determines your maximum payment with respect to your ratios. It does not take into account credit, credit score, loan programs, loan amounts or anything else.

QUICK PRE-QUALIFICATION

Following is a quick calculation that will give you a 'ballpark' idea as to the amount for which you qualify.

✓ Gross monthly income (before taxes)
(all borrowers combined): _____

✓ Multiply it by 49%   ___X_____.49

✓ Answer   _____

✓ Subtract the monthly payments
listed on your credit report   -_____

✓ **This number is the maximum**_____
monthly payment you will be able to handle by standard means of pre-qualification. This number *includes principal, interest, monthly taxes, monthly insurance and mortgage insurance, if applicable.* Ask the agent or loan officer to translate this into a home price for the area in which you want to buy.

Pre-Approval – A pre-approval runs the same computations as a pre-qualification, but also takes into account credit, credit score, loan programs, loan amounts and other applicable details.

To determine if you are pre-approved, the loan officer will take an application, run the information through the computer system and come up with an approval or denial. If it is approved, the loan officer can issue the pre-approval letter and also give you a list of documentation needed to complete the transaction.

After approval, the loan officer will be able to tell you the price range you can afford. This keeps you from finding a home you 'just can't live without' that is out of your price range. Trust me; this is the kind of information that is better to know sooner rather than later.

Pre-Approval Letter – A letter issued by the loan officer after your credit and financial situations have been analyzed. This letter states that you will be approved for the loan if all of the information you give to the loan officer turns out to be true and correct. Other supporting documentation like appraisals, inspections and the survey must be satisfactory too.

12

The Basics of Credit

Calculating the Score

Most people think if you pay your bills on time, your credit will be perfect. Wrong! Your credit score is not just a calendar tracking when you pay your bills. There is much more to it. Below is a ballpark idea for how they come up with your score. The number itself can range from 400 to 900 with a realistic range of 450 – 850.

Percentages of The Total Score

35% - Payment History - One of the most important things to a lender is your willingness and ability to pay your bills. That is why this category is the largest percentage of your score. The score is affected by how many bills have been paid late or sent to a collection agency and whether or not you have had any bankruptcies and/or foreclosures. The more recent these things are, the worse it is for your credit score. *Late rental or mortgage payments will really hurt your chances of getting a home loan.*

30% - Amount of Debt – This is the total amount of money you owe on all of your bills and loans. Credit cards with a high balance in relation to their maximum limit will lower your score. The more credit cards you have maxed out or nearly maxed out, the lower your score. The rule of thumb is to keep your card balances at 30% or less of their maximum limit.

15% - How Long You Have Had Credit – In a nutshell, the longer you have had established credit, the better your score will be.

10% - The Number Of Times Your Credit Is Checked – If your credit has been checked (also called an inquiry) frequently, it looks like you may be in financial trouble or taking on a lot of debt, so it decreases your score. Recent inquiries are worse for your score than older ones. The number of inquiries is counted on a 12 month basis. When you are shopping for a mortgage, you can have many inquiries from mortgage companies as long as they are within a 14 day period and they will not hurt your score.

10% - The Types Of Credit You Have – Types of credit means credit cards, mortgages, lines of credit, car loans, etc… This does not come into play too much unless you do not have enough credit on which to base a score.

Improving Your Score

Your credit score changes constantly because the information contained in it changes constantly. Below are some hints on improving your credit score.

Get a copy of your credit report and check it for errors. You would not believe how many mistakes you can find. Correcting these can improve you score – sometimes dramatically. Below are the three main credit reporting agencies. Call them and get a credit report from each one. You can get one per year, per agency – FREE. Below are the phone numbers and web addresses for each of the major credit reporting agencies.

Experian	Transunion	Equifax
888-397-3742	800-888-4213	800-685-1111
Experian.com	Transunion.com	Equifax.com

Do not close old credit card accounts. The ratio between actual debt and available debt is very important. Old cards that have available credit but no balance help your ratio.

The rule of thumb is to keep your card balances at 30% or less of their maximum limit. Also, make sure your credit card companies are reporting your true maximum credit limit and not just your current balance. If they are showing your current balance instead of maximum available credit, the report will show that you are maxed out on that card and hurt your score.

Pay your bills on time. (This is probably the most important of all!)

Catch up on all payments and pay off all collections and charge offs. Talk to a credit professional about paying off collections and charge offs if they are very old. Sometimes paying off old derogatory credit can hurt your score. (I don't agree with it either.)

Don't let anyone make an inquiry on your credit report unless you absolutely have too.

It takes time to improve your score. Take the needed steps and then wait 30 to 60 days. It will come up. Be patient.

If you are turned down for a loan, ask the loan officer for a list of reasons. You can use it as a laundry list for fixing your credit.

Remember, these are just tips. Consult a credit professional for coaching and advice.

13

Insurance Made Easy

Insurance, unfortunately, is necessary. In a nutshell, it makes sure that you are OK financially in case of an unfortunate mishap (storms, floods, fires, default on the loan, someone else claims your property etc…).

Insurance – *WARNING!* – There are several kinds of insurance with respect to a home purchase. It can get confusing.

> **Homeowner's** Covers the contents (furniture etc.) Not required by the lender, but very wise to have.
>
> **Hazard** Covers the home in case of fire and other hazards. Required for your loan.
>
> **Windstorm** Covers the home in case of hurricanes, tornados and the like. Required in some areas. Ask the lender.

Flood	Covers the home in case of floods. Required in some areas. Ask the lender.
Title	Insures that no one else has a claim to the property. Required by the lender.
Mortgage Insurance	Insures the bank against the borrower's failure to pay. It is Required if you have less than a 20% down payment and a single loan.

Mortgage Insurance – Also referred to as "MI, PMI, or MIP", insures the bank against the borrower's failure to pay. It is required if you have less than a 20% down payment and a single loan. Once you pay your loan balance to 80% of the current value of the house, you can usually request that it be dropped from your payment. Sometimes you have to wait at least two years, or depending on the program, meet other criteria too. When requesting that MI be dropped, you may have to get another appraisal to prove the current value of the house.

Mortgage insurance, if needed, will be included in your payment.

The terms "MI and PMI" are used in association with conventional loans and "MIP" is used in association with FHA loans.

How Do You Pay For Each Type Of Insurance?

Hazard, Windstorm and Flood Insurance are all paid, in advance, a year at a time. At closing you will be charged for one year's worth of insurance and several months worth of insurance payments to set up your escrow account (if necessary.)

Title Insurance is a one time fee paid at closing. Usually the seller will pay the majority of the cost, but not always.

Mortgage Insurance is paid monthly with your payment.

14

Types of Loans And Their Uses

CONVENTIONAL

A conventional loan is any loan that is not backed by a government entity such as FHA (Federal Housing Administration) or VA (Veterans Administration) and will be underwritten to FNMA (Federal National Mortgage Association) and FHLMC (Federal Home Loan Mortgage Corporation) guidelines. Borrowers must have acceptable credit scores and most collections and charge offs have to be paid off prior too or at closing. There is some leeway on the latter point, so ask your loan professional.

Following are examples of loans that are currently available and the situations to which they might apply.

Fixed Rate Mortgages – A fixed rate mortgage has an interest rate that is set for the life of the loan and never changes. Fixed rate loans are usually 10, 15, 20 and 30 years in length and are the most common type of loan. This is generally considered the best loan for people without any special goals or circumstances.

Adjustable Rate Mortgages – Also known as "variable rate mortgages" and "ARMs", these loans have an interest rate that changes during the life of the loan. At the beginning of the loan, they almost always have a lower interest rate than the standard fixed rate mentioned above. The interest rate can move up and down over time and probably will.

ARMs are a great strategy in specific situations and can save you lots of money or help you start saving for retirement. ARMs are not for everyone or every situation. Discuss this type of mortgage in detail with your loan officer before making your decision. (See Chapter 15 for a much more thorough explanation)

Balloons – Balloons are short term loans, usually 3, 5, 7 or 10 years. The payments, however, are calculated as if they are a 30 year mortgage. The interest rate is fixed for the life of the loan and is usually lower than the current thirty year fixed rate. At the end of the term (3, 5, 7 or 10 years), the entire balance of the note is due. If you are not ready to pay off the loan at that time, you will have to either refinance or sell the home. These loans are good for people who will only live in their home for a few years.

Interest Only Loan – A loan program where you pay only the interest portion of the payment and not the principal. This is usually only for a relatively short period of time after which you will need to pay off the loan or start making principal payments. Interest only loans are primarily used to lower the mortgage payments during the first few years. It does not lower it as much as you would think and the interest rate is usually higher than the same loan without the interest only feature. Interest only loans are primarily used by people who will be paying off their loan quickly.

First and Second - When you get two loans instead of one, it is called a first and second. The "first" is the biggest loan, usually with an 80% loan-to-value or less. The "second" is the smaller loan and is usually has a 10% - 20% loan-to-value. If you add the two numbers together, you get the "combined loan to value". However, since each loan is less than 80% of the price of the home, you do not need mortgage insurance and it is optional to have your taxes and insurance included in the monthly payment.

The "first" sometimes has a slightly higher than normal interest rate and the "second", since it is in a riskier position than the first, has a much higher interest rate. The two payments together, however, usually come out lower than the payment on one loan with mortgage insurance. Following is an illustration.

Price: $200,000
Loan Amount: $190,000
Term: 30 years
Interest rate on the 1st lien is 6%
Interest rate on the 2nd lien is 7.5%
Payments are monthly Principal and Interest payments only
Mortgage Insurance is quoted in terms of a monthly payment

One Loan		**First and Second (2 loans)**	
Payment	$1139	Payment on 1st	$959
Mortgage Insurance	$124	Payment on 2nd	$210
Total	$1263		$1169
Difference		**$94 per month**	

The terms "first" and "second" come from the lien position on the property. The "first" has the first lien and the "second" has a second lien. If the borrower fails to make the payments, the house will be taken back by the lender and sold to pay off the loan. The first lien is paid off first and whatever is left over goes to pay off the second lien. Hopefully, the sales price of the home is enough to pay off both liens. If there is not enough money generated by the sale of the property to pay off the second lien, the lender may have to take it as a loss. Since interest is paid for risk, it makes sense that the second lien has a higher interest rate. Its chances of getting paid off are less and, therefore, it is a riskier position for the lender.

Notation of a first and second is unusual until you get familiar with it. Following are examples:

80/15/5   80/10/10   70/20/10

The first number is the loan to value of the "first" loan. The second number is the loan to value of the "second" loan and the third number is the down payment.

If you see 80/20, that is a first and second with no down payment. 80+20=100% so, there is no need for a down payment.

Documentation Types – Conventional

Due to unusual circumstances that life sometimes offers, there are differing documentation types available. Keep in mind that each time you go outside of the "full doc box", the interest rate goes up. As you go down the following list, the interest rate and minimum credit score will usually increase.

Full Doc – This stands for "Full Documentation". Everything is needed. Pay stubs, tax returns, bank statements, verification of employment, employment history, asset verification, W-2 or 1099 and more. (See Chapter 6)

Stated Income – Self employed borrowers and people with many assets and bank accounts use this. With this program you only have to state your income, not prove it with W-2s, 1099s or tax returns. You do have to verify assets. Proof of employment, usually 2 years, is required too.

Stated Income/Stated Assets – With this program you simply state your income and assets and do not have to prove them. Proof of employment, usually 2 years, is required.

No Income/No Assets – With this program you do not have to state or prove your income or assets. Proof of employment may be required.

No Ratio – With this program the ratio concerning debt to income is not calculated. In fact, no income or debts are stated. Proof of employment may be required.

No Doc/Verified Assets – With this program no employment is stated or verified but assets have to be verified.

No Doc – With this program there is no documentation required.

GOVERNMENT

There are two types of government loans, FHA and VA. This means that they are insured by either the Federal Housing Administration or Veterans Administration.

FHA

FHA loans require little down payment and are amortized over 15 or 30 years. The down payment can be a gift and closing costs are reduced for the buyer because the government mandates that the buyer not pay certain items. These types of loans are more lenient than conventional loans with respect to credit score and you do not have to repay charge offs or collections that appear on your credit report before you close.

There are two types of mortgage insurance with FHA loans. The first is the Up Front Mortgage Insurance Premium. This has to be paid at closing no matter what. The second is monthly Mortgage Insurance Premium "MIP". This is the one that is part of your payment. Following is a summary of the details concerning MIP.

MIP Details Of An FHA Loan
(The following examples are for monthly MIP only, not Up Front MIP.
Up Front MIP is a one time charge that is paid at closing.)

30 year loans: MIP is .5% of the initial base loan amount. That number is divided by 12 and put into your monthly payment. MIP will stay on the loan for a minimum of 5 years AND will remain until the balance drops below 78% of the original purchase price.

15 year loans: MIP is .25% of the initial base loan amount. That number is divided by 12 and put into your monthly payment. It will stay in the monthly payment until the loan balance drops below 78% of the original purchase price. There is not a time limit on the 15 year loan. One way to get out of paying MIP is to pay 10% + $1 or more as a down payment. You must, however, pay MIP with the purchase of condominiums or rehabilitation projects no matter how much you put down as a down payment.

VA

These loans are for active military and military veterans. The biggest benefits are that no down payment or mortgage insurance is required. There is a "funding fee" charged at closing by the VA that is unavoidable unless you have a disability. It is a percentage of the loan amount and changes depending on the down payment, if any, and a number of times the borrower's VA entitlement has been used. Closing costs on VA loans are reduced for the buyer because the government mandates that the buyer not pay certain items.

These types of loans are more lenient than conventional loans with respect to credit score and you do not have to repay charge offs or collections that appear on your credit report before you close.

Eligibility for a VA loan depends on the discharge papers, DD-214, and a calculation that figures residuals. Your loan officer can crunch those numbers for you. The VA office that covers your area will issue a certificate of eligibility if you are eligible for a VA loan.

SUB-PRIME

These loans are for people who have credit problems or other very unique situations which make FHA, VA and Conventional loans difficult or impossible to get. The interest rate is usually much higher than conventional, FHA or VA loan programs. Most of the time they do not require mortgage insurance or escrows for taxes and insurance (the situation where your monthly tax and insurance payments are included with your payment).

The companies that offer sub-prime loans utilize both fixed and adjustable rate mortgages. The short term adjustable rate mortgages offer the cheapest interest rates. A strategy that is frequently used with sub-prime loans is to get into the loan for two years or so and during that time clean up your credit. When the pre-payment penalty period is up, you refinance into a conventional loan with a lower interest rate.

The adjustable rate loans offered by these companies come in the form of the 2/28, 3/27 etc... The first number is the number of years the interest rate is fixed and the second number is the number of years the interest rate will adjust. The rate will usually only adjust one time per year. (See the Chapter 15 for more detail on ARMs)

15

Adjustable Rate Mortgages (ARMs)

There are many different types of ARMs that serve many different purposes. Below is a summary of the most common adjustable rate mortgages available today.

FIXED TERM ARMs – Fixed term ARMs are fantastic for people who know they will only live in the home for a few years or will pay off the loan quickly.

The interest rate for the initial period of these loans is fixed and in many cases lower than the 30 year fixed rate loan. The notation used in the name of these loans tells two things; how many years the fixed rate period lasts and how often the interest rate will change after the fixed rate period is over.

Loan Name	Years The Interest Rate is Fixed	How Often The Rate Adjusts After Fixed Period
1/1	1 year	Yearly for 29 years
3/1	3 years	Yearly for 27 years

5/1	5 years	Yearly for 25 years
7/1	7 years	Yearly for 23 years
10/1	10 years	Yearly for 20 years

Most fixed period ARMs can be done as "interest only" loans too.

All ARMs have interest rate caps. There will usually be three rate caps. They will be noted as 5/2/5, 2/2/5 etc... The first number is the maximum percent that the interest rate can change the first time it changes. The second number is the maximum percent that the interest rate can change in any one year period. The last number is the lifetime maximum interest rate change.

Following is an example:
3/1 ARM with 5/2/5 caps - Assume the starting interest rate is 3%. It will stay at 3% for 3 years. When it changes the first time, it can go up a **maximum** of 5% to a total of 8%.

In this example 8% happens to be the maximum *first change* cap as well as the *lifetime* interest rate cap – 3%+5% = 8%. If the rate, however, does not increase the maximum amount on the first interest rate change, it still has room to increase and can do so at a maximum rate of 2% per year until it hits 8% - the lifetime interest rate cap.

Sub-Prime Fixed Period Arms
Fixed period ARMs in the Sub-Prime category are similar to the 3/1 ARM mentioned above except they have different names. They are known as the 2/28 and 3/27. Below is a description of each.

Loan Name	Years the Interest Rate is Fixed	How Often Rate Adjusts After Fixed Period
2/28	2 years	Yearly for 28 years
3/27	3 years	Yearly for 27 years

ARMs are confusing at first. Ask questions and keep asking until you understand.

PAY OPTION ARM

If you are **sophisticated financially** and have **very good financial habits**, this may be the loan for you. If used correctly, this loan can make available to you sizeable sums of cash that can be used in any manner you choose. The most common uses are; paying off debt, setting up retirement, and investing.

Following is the basic premise of the pay option ARM. For the first five years or so, you are allowed to make a minimum payment that slowly increases over time and is far below the current market interest rate. This makes money available to you each month that you would normally have to pay toward your loan.

Each month during the first five years or so you will be able to pick your payment from the following choices; minimum payment, interest only, 30 year payoff, 15 year payoff and anything in between.

WARNING!!! These are the loans that are advertised with a "1% interest rate" or "$200,000 loan with a monthly payment for less than your car payment" or "$200,000 loan for just $600 per month" etc... What they are not telling you is that it is just for a short time, sometimes just one month, and that your loan balance can, and probably will, grow over time instead of decrease.

What you encounter with these "great low rates" is deferred interest. This happens when you choose to pay the minimum payment and it does not cover all of the interest that is due. The portion of interest that is not paid is added to your loan balance.

There are some fantastic financial uses for this loan, but you have to be disciplined and know what you are doing. If you are not completely comfortable with the concept and fully aware of all of the loan details, do not do it.

Discuss this loan thoroughly with your loan officer before entering into it.

16

Condominiums and Townhouses

Condominiums and Townhouses are very similar. With each one, you buy an individual unit that is usually attached to other units and part of a larger complex. You will probably only own the interior of the unit, not the exterior. Most of the time, the common areas and exterior of the buildings are owned by everyone and they are maintained by the Home Owner's Association. The Home Owner's Association will collect fees, usually monthly, in order to have money for maintenance and repairs of the common areas.

With townhouses, you own the land directly beneath the unit and with condos the association owns it. Townhouses will have separate addresses and condos will have one address with different unit numbers.

Condominiums and Townhouses are so similar that, many times, you cannot tell which form a property takes without looking up the legal documents used to create it.

THINGS TO WATCH

When it comes to getting a mortgage for condominiums, have your real estate agent research the following items and inform the loan officer. Do this up front because it can destroy a deal if left until the end. None of the following applies to townhouses – they are just like purchasing a regular home.

How many stories is the property? If it is over 4 or 5 you may have a problem getting financing.

What percentage of the units are rented out? This one is REALLY important.

Does the property have a front check in desk for rental units?

Do they offer daily, weekly or monthly rentals?

Is there any space on the property dedicated to commercial use i.e. restaurants, gift shops, etc...? If so, what percentage of the total square footage is devoted to commercial uses.

The answers to the questions above will dictate to the lender whether or not the property is considered a non-warrantable condo or a condo-hotel (condotel). If it is, you may have to settle for a much higher down payment and interest rate.

Check these things out first so there is no big surprise at the end.

17

Investment Properties

When you are buying a property as an investment, you are planning on renting it out and/or waiting for the property to appreciate in value. Below are some key things to know.

The less money you use for a down payment, the higher your interest rate. You can go with 'no money down' but the rate will probably kill any chances of positive cash flow on the property. If you put 25% or more down, you will get the best rate. Usually, 25% down will get as good an interest rate as putting more money down.

There are significant tax advantages to owning investment property. Contact your CPA to discuss them in detail

Visit with an insurance agent who is used to dealing with investment properties and discuss all types of insurance that may apply. This is very important because there are many different insurance products available to meet the wide range of needs the investor may have.

When calculating cash flow, take into account more than just the monthly payment. Look at taxes, insurance, maintenance, repairs and any other items of which you and your CPA can think.

18

Earnest Money vs. Down Payment

EARNEST MONEY

This is the money, usually a check, which you send along with your offer to buy the house. It shows the buyer that you are serious. In the old days, earnest money was not refundable, but today you may have an option period and, if you exercise your option within the given time period, you can probably get your earnest money back.

When the contract is agreed too by both parties, the agent will take it, along with your earnest money check, to the title company. They will hold it until the deal closes. You will get credit for the earnest money at closing.

DOWN PAYMENT

This is part of the money you will pay "out of pocket" at closing. It is usually much more than the earnest money.

Your down payment plus the loan amount should equal the price of the home. Discuss this thoroughly with your lender.

19

Inspections vs. Appraisals

APPRAISALS

An appraisal is an opinion of current market value for a home. It is usually done by an independent appraiser and is normally required by the lender. Sometimes an appraisal may indicate that repairs are needed. These are known as "lender required repairs" and must be done in order to get the loan. An appraiser does not do a detailed inspection like an official "Property Inspector" does.

Your loan amount will be calculated on the lower of the contract price or appraised value. This can make a big difference!

Following are examples of how your loan can be affected by an appraisal that comes in low as opposed to one that comes in at value.

"At Value" Appraisal

Contract Price	$100,000
Appraised Value	$100,000
Loan To Value	95%

Down Payment	$5,000
Loan Amount	$95,000
Monthly Payment (w/o tax and insurance)	$567
Cash Required For Closing	$5,000
plus closing costs and pre-paid expenses	

"Below Value" Appraisal

Contract Price	$100,000
Appraised Value	**$ 90,000**
Loan To Value	95%

Down Payment	$4,500
Loan Amount	$85,500
Monthly Payment (w/o tax and insurance)	$513
Cash Required For Closing	**$14,500**
plus closing costs and pre-paid expenses	

The extra $10,000 in the "Cash required for closing" calculation comes from the difference between the sales price and appraised value. The seller still wants $100,000 but the lender will only loan $85,500.

When an appraisal comes in low, there are four things that can happen.
1. The seller must drop his price to the appraised value.
2. The buyer must bring enough money to closing to make up the difference between the appraised value and contract price.
3. The buyer and seller meet somewhere in the middle.
4. The deal dies.

INSPECTIONS

It is your option whether or not to hire an inspector. In my personal experience, I have been happy every time I have had an inspection done. A good inspector will go over the property with a 'fine tooth comb' and find just about anything that might be wrong with it. They will give you a lengthy report that describes the type and location of problems and suggestions on ways to remedy them. Many times the report will include pictures in the problem description. Inspectors will not give an opinion of value and are not usually required by the lender.

Use common sense when reading these reports. The inspection business is so filled with liability that they word everything in the report to make it sound as if it is in the worst condition possible. I have seen home purchases fall through because the inspector described the *rose bushes* in such a menacing manner that the buyers got scared and backed out of the contract. Use your own judgment and common sense.

TERMITE INSPECTIONS

Sometimes, depending on the lender and type of loan, a termite inspection is required. An independent company will visit the property and deliver a report detailing the termite problem, if any. If there is a problem it will need to be corrected before closing.

20

Pre-Paid Interest Made Simple

Key Points to Understanding The Following Diagram

1. Monthly house payments pay interest that is due for the preceding month. For example, a payment made at the beginning of August will pay the interest due for July.

2. The first payment made on a home comes at the beginning of the second month. For example, if a person closes in June, the first payment will be due in August.

3. The borrower will start owing interest at the time the loan is closed and funded. The borrower will never pay interest for any time they do not have the funds.

4. The later in the month a loan closes, the less the amount of pre-paid interest that must be paid at closing.

Quick Summary

Study the chart below and see how the interest not paid by the first payment is paid at closing. It is called "Pre-paid" Interest because it is paid before it is due.

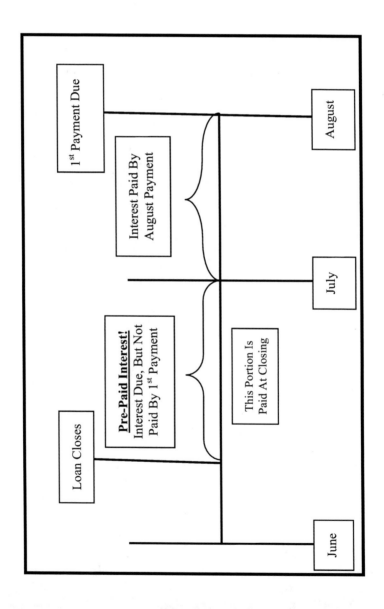

21

Definitions

These definitions may not be as described in a dictionary. They are in terms of everyday language and usage.

APR

This stands for "Annual Percentage Rate". This is a government mandated calculation that takes into account most of the costs associated with the loan and spreads them out over time. **It is not your interest rate.** You are looking for an APR that is close to the actual interest rate.

Appraisal

A report compiled by an appraiser that indicates the market value of the property. The appraiser usually inspects the property, finds recent sales in the area that are similar to the property being appraised, crunches the numbers and comes up with a value. If the appraisal comes in below the contract sales price, you have problems. Talk to your real estate agent and loan officer quickly. If it comes in at the contract sales price, everything is great. If it comes in above the sales price, you are doing well because you have instant equity.

Appreciation
An increase in property value over time.

Cash Flow – The movement of cash into and out of your investment. A positive cash flow means you are making a profit and a negative cash flow means you are losing money.

Closing
Closing is the last step in the transaction. It can be done in front of a notary public or at a title company. It is where all of the paper work is signed, the final check is delivered by the buyer and funds are transferred to the seller. Closing can take place in person or be done via overnight mail.

Closing Costs – *WARNING!*
In everyday language, "closing costs" has several meanings. Use the terms correctly and start thinking as such. The most correct usage is the "lenders" definition below.

<u>Various Possible Meanings</u>
To normal borrowers, "closing costs" means;
1. All costs + down payment.
2. All money you need to bring to closing.
To lenders, "closing costs" means;
All bank fees and fees from outside of the bank. This does not take into account prepaid expenses (taxes and insurance) or down payment.
To sly internet companies, "closing costs" means; a select few bank fees only and leaves out EVERYTHING else.

Collateral

Anything of value pledged to the lender to secure the loan. It is usually the home itself. If you default on your loan the bank takes the collateral and sells it to get enough money to pay off the loan and all expenses.

Combined Loan To Value

Also known as CLTV, combined loan to value is when there are two loans for a property and both of the loans-to-value are added together. (See loan to value)

Condominium

This is an individual unit in a multi-unit structure. The owner owns the inside of the unit, not the outside or land.

Condo Hotel

Also known as a "condotel", a condo hotel is a condominium with a rental desk and/or commercial space on the property.

Conventional Loan
Standard loan that is not insured by government sources and is underwritten to conform to Fannie Mae or Freddie Mac guidelines.

Default
If you fail to make payments on your mortgage, you are in default and the bank may take your home and sell it to pay off the loan. Don't get into default. Nothing good comes from it. (See foreclosure)

Deferred interest
The case where your monthly payment is not covering all of the interest that is due and the portion that is not paid is added to your loan balance.

Depreciation
A decrease in property value over time.

Down Payment
Also known as "down" - The "out of pocket" money you pay toward the price of the property.

Example:
Price	$100,000
Loan Amount	- 80,000
Down Payment	$ 20,000

Easement
Right-of-way that allows for access to the property by certain interested parties. For example; the utility company may need to periodically have access to the property to work on utility equipment.

Earnest Money

Money you include with your offer to buy the house. It shows that you are serious and it will be credited toward the down payment or costs associated with the loan when you close. It is possible to either loose your earnest money or have it refunded during the home buying process. Ask your real estate agent about the conditions.

Equity

The money you could put in your pocket if you sold the house and paid off the loan.

Example:
Sales Price $200,000
Loan to be paid off $150,000
Equity $ 50,000

Escrow – WARNING!!!

There are several definitions for this word. Be careful and ask questions. (See impounds)

Definitions of "escrow"
with Respect To Different Uses

Contract – When the contract and earnest money are placed at the title company the contract is said to be "escrowed" or held in escrow.

Loan – When your money is used to get tax and insurance accounts set up. The accounts that are set up are known as "escrow accounts."

Escrow Process

At closing you will have to "escrow" a certain amount of money for taxes and insurance (usually 2 months insurance payments and 3 to 4 months tax payments). This means the bank will create special accounts with this money and you will add to them each month by way of your monthly payment. When your tax and insurance bills become due, the bank uses the money in these accounts to pay the bills. You do not pay it, the bank does it for you. You do not have to escrow if you have 20% down or two loans. Ask your loan officer about this.

FHA Loan
A loan insured by the Federal Housing Administration.

FHLMC
Also known as "Freddie Mac", the Federal Home Loan Mortgage Corporation is a Government-chartered corporation that buys qualified mortgage loans from financial institutions and sells them through the dealer community.

FNMA
Also known as "Fannie Mae", the Federal National Mortgage Association is a corporation which buys mortgages on the secondary market, pools them and sells them as mortgage-backed securities to investors on the open market.

Foreclosure
Foreclosure is when the lender takes back the property after the buyer has defaulted.

Home Equity Line Of Credit
Also known as a "Line of Credit" or "HELOC". This is similar to the Cash Out Refinance except that you do not pay off the current loan. With this loan product, the bank allows you to borrow a predetermined amount of

money. You do not have to take it all at once and can take it in little bits and pay it back in little bits. It is almost like a credit card with your home securing the payment. Discuss HELOCs in detail with your lender.

Impounds

Impounds are also known as escrows. This is when monthly tax and insurance payments are included with your monthly mortgage payment.

Inspection

Inspections are oftentimes confused with the appraisal. An inspection simply tells you what is wrong with the home. It does not give value and is much more detailed than the appraisal. Inspections are not required by the lender, but it is wise to get one.

Insurance – *WARNING!*

There are several kinds of insurance with respect to a home purchase. It can get confusing.

Homeowner's Covers the contents (furniture etc.) Not required for your loan.

Hazard Required for your loan – covers the home in case of fire and other hazards.

Windstorm Covers the home in case of hurricanes, tornados and the like. Required in some areas. Ask the lender.

Flood Covers the home in case of floods. Required in some areas. Ask the lender.

Title Insures that no one else has a claim to the property. Required by the lender.

Mortgage Insurance

Insures the bank against the borrower's failure to pay. It is required if you have less than a 20% down payment and a single loan.

Lender Required Repairs

If the appraisal notes items in the home need to be repaired, they are considered "lender required" and must be done before closing. Negotiations determine whether the buyer, seller or both will pay for them.

Lien

A lien is a claim against the property for money. If someone is owed money and is not paid by the owner, the person that is owed the money can put a lien on the house. This means that when the property is sold, that person will get paid from the proceeds of the sale. There are many different types of liens and they will need to be settled at or before closing.

Loan To Value

Also known as "LTV", the loan to value is a percentage that states what portion of the price is paid by the loan. For example;

Loan Amount $80,000
Price $100,000
$80,000 / $100,000 = 80%
Loan to Value = 80%

Mortgage

A home loan.

Mortgage Insurance

Also referred to as "MI, PMI, or MIP", insures the bank against the borrower's failure to pay. It is required if you have less than 20% down as a down payment and a single loan. Once you pay your loan balance to 80% of the current value_of the house, you can request that it be dropped and, usually, it will. Sometimes you have to wait at least two years. When requesting that MI be dropped, you may have to get another appraisal to prove the current value of the house.

Mortgage insurance will be included in your payment.

The terms "MI and PMI" will be used in association with conventional loans and "MIP" will be used in association with FHA loans.

Mortgagee

The lender. The one to whom the collateral is pledged to secure the loan.

Mortgagor

You, the one who pledges the property as collateral to secure the loan.

Non-Warrantable Condominium

A non-warrantable condominium is a condominium that does not conform to Fannie Mae standards and is, therefore, not eligible for any loan that is sold under Fannie Mae guidelines.

Option Period

A period agreed to in the contract that lets you do inspections and almost anything else you need to do to make sure you want to complete the purchase. The option period will usually cost a nominal fee. In most cases it allows for the return of your earnest money should you back out of the deal during the given time period. This is also known as a feasibility period.

Origination Fee

Fee charged by the bank to pay the loan officer and expenses. (Loan officers need to feed their families too. It also adds to their motivation and that is ALWAYS a good thing.)

PITI Payment

No this is not a comment on how bad your mortgage payment is - it is an acronym. It stands for Principal, Interest, Taxes and Insurance. It is your entire monthly home loan payment. *It does leave out mortgage insurance*, though.

Points

Fee paid by the borrower to the lender. Usually, points are paid to lower the interest rate or increase tax advantages. Sometimes, they are just extra money in the bank's pockets.

Pre-Approval Letter

A letter issued by the loan officer stating you are pre-approved for the loan based on credit, a survey, appraisal and other supporting documentation.

"Pre-Paid" Expenses

This is money that must be paid at closing to set up your tax and insurance accounts with the bank. It also pays any portion of pre-paid interest that is due.

Pre-Paid Interest

This is Interest that is due on your loan but will not be covered by the first payment. (See Chapter 20 for more details)

Pre-Payment Penalty

A pre-payment penalty is a financial penalty that is charged to the borrower if the loan is paid off within a given time period. Usually it is 1 – 5 years. Ask your loan officer if there is a pre-payment penalty and, if there is, discuss the matter thoroughly.

Prime loans

Also known as "A" paper loans, these loans are designed for people with good credit.

Rate Locks

This is a tool that loan officers use to fix the rate while the loan is in process. Lengthy rate locks – over 45 days – can cost you money or cause you to have a higher interest rate. Be careful and ask questions!

Refinance

A refinance is when you get a new loan that pays off and takes the place of your current home loan. There two types of refinances, Cash Out (also known as a home equity loan) and a Rate and Term.

Cash Out Refinance – This is when you borrow more than you owe and keep the money that is left over after the current loan and expenses are paid off. You are taking 'cash out' of your current home.

Rate and Term Refinance – This is when you borrow enough to pay off your existing loan plus associated expenses and do not have cash left over.

Sub-Prime loans

Also known as "B" and "C" paper loans, these loans are designed for people with credit problems or out of the ordinary situations.

Survey

This is a drawing of the property that shows the exact property lines and the locations of all structures contained within them. They also show building lines, easements, etc...

Title

The title policy is an insurance policy that guarantees no one else has a claim of ownership to your property. It will also show any liens, easements, etc...that affect the property.

Townhouse

A townhouse is one unit in a multi-unit property. The owner has title to the interior of the unit and the land beneath it.

VA Loan

A loan that is available to active military or veterans that is guaranteed by the government. There is not any down payment or mortgage insurance required.

22

Summary

The home buying experience can be very pleasant if you take your time and select the right loan officer and real estate agent. Work hand in hand with them while being as honest and loyal as possible. They will serve you and guide you through the process. In the end, you will relax in your new home and start enjoying this new chapter in your life.

May God bless you and America!!!

Appendix A

How To Contact The Author And Bigger Picture Publishing

I would love to hear your comments. Please contact me by any of the methods listed below.

Email:
ultimatehomebuyersbook@yahoo.com

Phone:
800-221-5040

Mail:
Bigger Picture Publishing
PMB 394
14493 SPID
Corpus Christi, TX 78418

MCE Classes For Real Estate Agents:
See Following Page

SPEAKING AVAILABILITY
Wade Grassedonio is available for speaking engagements. If you would like him to speak at a function, please make your request via email or phone.

CONTINUING EDUCATION CLASSES FOR REAL ESTATE AGENTS

Wade Grassedonio is approved to teach the material in this book as an MCE class in Texas.

The title of the class is:
Buyers, Agents & Lenders; Strategies for Success
4 hours, non-legal

Classes can be held at any location in Texas.
To schedule a class at your location, call the author.

800-221-5040

ORDER FORM

Price Per Copy $9.99

Number of Copies   _____
Sub Total   _____
Texas Residents Add $ 0.87 _____
        sales tax **per book**
Shipping/Postage $3.00   1st book,
                          $1.50   each additional book
Total   _____

Please send my order to (print clearly):
Name:_____
Street Address:_____

_____
City, St., Zip:_____
Phone:_____
Email:_____

Payment Method (circle one): check, money order, credit card
MasterCard or Visa (circle one)
Card Number: _____
Exp. Date: _____
Name on card: _____

Signature:

_____

Internet Orders: www.ultimatehomebuyersbook.com
Email Order: ultimatehomebuyersbook@yahoo.com
Toll Free Orders: 800-221-5040
Fax Order: 361-949-1522
Mail Orders To: Bigger Picture Publishing
                     PMB 394
                     14493 SPID
                     Corpus Christi, TX 78418

ORDER FORM

Price Per Copy $9.99

Number of Copies   _____
Sub Total   _____
Texas Residents Add $ 0.87 _____
    sales tax **per book**
Shipping/Postage $3.00 1st book,
                                       $1.50 each additional book
Total   _____

Please send my order to (print clearly):
Name:_____
Street Address:_____
_____
City, St., Zip:_____
Phone:_____
Email:_____

Payment Method (circle one)**:** check, money order, credit card
MasterCard or Visa (circle one)
Card Number: _____
Exp. Date: _____
Name on card: _____

Signature:
_____

Internet Orders: www.ultimatehomebuyersbook.com
Email Order: ultimatehomebuyersbook@yahoo.com
Toll Free Orders: 800-221-5040
Fax Order: 361-949-1522
Mail Orders To: Bigger Picture Publishing
                        PMB 394
                        14493 SPID
                        Corpus Christi, TX 78418

<u>ORDER FORM</u>

Price Per Copy $9.99

Number of Copies   _____
Sub Total   _____
Texas Residents Add $ 0.87   _____
     sales tax **per book**
Shipping/Postage $3.00   1st book,
                                            $1.50   each additional book
Total   _____

Please send my order to (print clearly):
Name:_____
Street Address:_____

_____
City, St., Zip:_____
Phone:_____
Email:_____

Payment Method (circle one): check, money order, credit card
MasterCard or Visa (circle one)
Card Number: _____
Exp. Date: _____
Name on card: _____

Signature:

_____

Internet Orders: www.ultimatehomebuyersbook.com
Email Order: ultimatehomebuyersbook@yahoo.com
Toll Free Orders: 800-221-5040
Fax Order: 361-949-1522
Mail Orders To: Bigger Picture Publishing
                            PMB 394
                            14493 SPID
                            Corpus Christi, TX 78418

ORDER FORM

Price Per Copy	$9.99
Number of Copies	_____
Sub Total	_____
Texas Residents Add $ 0.87	_____
sales tax **per book**	
Shipping/Postage	$3.00 1st book,
	$1.50 each additional book
Total	_____

Please send my order to (print clearly):

Name:_____

Street Address:_____

_____

City, St., Zip:_____

Phone:_____

Email:_____

Payment Method (circle one): check, money order, credit card

MasterCard or Visa (circle one)

Card Number: _____

Exp. Date: _____

Name on card: _____

Signature:

_____

Internet Orders: www.ultimatehomebuyersbook.com

Email Order: ultimatehomebuyersbook@yahoo.com

Toll Free Orders: 800-221-5040

Fax Order: 361-949-1522

Mail Orders To: Bigger Picture Publishing
PMB 394
14493 SPID
Corpus Christi, TX 78418

Notes

Notes